Decoding Thoughts and Inner Voice. Explanations and Debunking the Misconceptions.

By

David Gomadza

Founder President

Tomorrow's World Order

ISBN: 9798801455488
Imprint: Independently published

It is a challenge to decode thoughts and the inner voice. Hence the need for an equally challenging invention to match. As a lot of issues must be addressed. Does this book and the first book: Thoughts to Word or Audio effectively address the following obstacles to decoding thoughts.

Misunderstanding of the human system.

The complexity of the brain as a hindrance to the decoding of thoughts.

The need to record both in space and time and the shortfalls of all current methods.

The brain's ability to process 600 thoughts per minute and the inability of the current methods to address this.

A lack of a holistic approach to decoding thoughts.

Misunderstanding of the structure and mechanism of the brain.

Other things, like emotions and other experiences, can't be explained by simply looking at brain activity and neuron activity.

Explanations and debunking the misconceptions.

DEDICATION

To an exciting New Word Order spearheaded by Tomorrow's World Order.

This book must be read after reading the first book; Thoughts to Word or Audio. How To Know Exactly What Someone Is Thinking.

CONTENTS

ACKNOWLEDGMENTS

Special Thanks to Tomorrow's World Order.

CHAPTER ONE

I argued in the first book that to be able to decode what a person is thinking at a given time, a different approach must be adopted. One where the shift is from looking for the area where the brain activity occurs, to the need to identify what neurons were firing at a particular point in both space and time. I argued that this is possible if you incorporate the delayed time-space continuum mechanism that stipulates that it is possible to revisit a place and point in time and manipulate the situation to replay exactly what happened then but now so that current events can be superimposed on top of that event and all recorded as if all just happened at that point in time.

In the first book; Thoughts to Word or Audio, for argument's sake, I introduced some weird working hypotheses but one relevant here is one that states that it is possible to employ a technique called word-search. A situation where a person is given a recreated scenario in order to make the person say words we want to hear and record these then use the delayed time-space technique to revert to a point in time and superimpose what we have recorded through the use of word-search. Then superimpose on events revisited events that had already happened, then record the two as if both were happening at that moment in time.

For example, a fight between lovers where the man's word-searched words are used. Ones which were obtained somehow for example, where he was made angry and due to the pain at the time, cursed hard, threatening to kill the abuser then the cursings are recorded and mixed with the scene visited in time when he fought with his wife making it look like he was threatening his girlfriend to anyone who hears the recordings. With the woman ending up disappearing, etc.

The advantage of this method of superimposing two situations together as above is that it make it possible to record the first person's voice, events, speech, and the brain light wave pattern or shape as well as the shape of the sound waves at the specific point, place and time then decode these as a sample. Then go back to that point and make the third person be synchronized to the subject and everything recreated with the third person's brain light waves pattern, sound wave pattern, and everything else recorded and both compared to be able to compare and decode what the person heard as inner voice and his thoughts, etc at that point and place in time.. This can be repeated until the results all match.

In short, this delayed time-space continuum enables the recreation of exact situations and replay them over and over again until you have a definite answer and accurate decoding of events, thoughts, and what transpired at that point.

CHAPTER TWO

I made some working assumptions even though I believe that they are facts but just for argument's sake to keep an open mind and give you a chance to rethink all this and contribute as well.

I believe that the human body has two systems, one which we know and a hidden internal one, one that works in opposite or in reverse. Meaning that there is an internal microphone, speaker, brain, transducers or wave converter, etc and a hint to this is the inner voice.

A human body is a perfect system, we know that every perfect system according to Newton's laws has two forces: a direct force with an equal but opposing force. That means every outward force, be it a sound wave, is accompanied by an opposite but equal force that operates in the other direction as an inward force. This means two waves are produced each time we speak but the other one is converted into a different but equal wave form meaning into light waves that are equal as they occupy the same area of the brain and often (another working assumption) have the same pattern. So, when a sound wave is an output wave, then light waves of the same magnitude or frequency are input to the inner system.

The body needs and has several transducers that automatically convert different waves into several forms to send one outward and the other inward to the internal system at the same time as a way to balance the perfect system. For example, sound waves go out when we speak, but these same waves are converted instantly to light waves as an equal but opposing force that goes inward to the second inner secret system. But when the light waves reach the internal secret system of the body, the processes are reversed and then continued. Now the light waves are converted back to sound waves from the inner secret system to the human system. The very thing you know as the inner voice. The very reason why we hear the voice in our heads. Since the brain can only act on our own voice when the light waves are converted to sound waves a language we can understand, we hear our voice (inner voice) as the sound inside can only be ours. This is true in that if a voice of a person is replayed to that person deep in the ear as the person is sleeping, the body converts that artificial inner voice into the dreams of that person. But if someone's voice is replayed in the deep ear as the person is sleeping, that person might not dream about that and might wake up scared and shaken.

In addition the method assumes it is possible to synthesize speech from brain neural activity patterns. Through simulated movements of the vocal tract to generate speech. Sound wave patterns when thinking without talking are similar to spoken language ones. The invention will therefore enable the collection of data and samples over time to create a definite way of decoding thoughts and inner voice by creating reference stencils to use to decode thoughts.

My invention is based on the idea that we need three but all linked systems in each human body to be able to decode thoughts and inner voices, even dreams. The body's perfect system, therefore, must include the system we know, its inner hidden secret system, and an additional artificial digital inside-system that imitates and is synchronized to the body's own inner secret system, which the inner voice is part of. That brings me to the next point.

For any serious people in robotics who want to create a robot that can be like a human being, they must input or use three or even more digital life systems just in one robot, see Fig 1. If humans are alive and clever as they are because of multiple systems inside them, then it is absurd to just use one human system in robots. Would you be surprised that there are no clever robots? But it's not just inputting the three systems inside robots, but creating a viciously-linked and continuous cycle with equal and opposing systems. One that has transducers that converts waves to different forms depending on their direction of movements whether inward or outward. If sound waves are outputted, then the same waves are converted to light waves as part of electromagnetic waves and inputted. But when light waves reach inside, they are converted back in the inner secret system back to us as sound waves. The inner voice we hear.

We don't hear inner voices when we speak because the light waves are converted to electromagnetic waves that are absorbed inside with only weak vibrations being outputted.

But an interesting point to note here is that when we think but not speak that means there are no sound waves produced so two sets of light waves are produced that go both to the inner system with one converted to electromagnetic waves that are absorbed and the other reverted to our system as sound waves. The inner voice we can hear.

I argued that if anyone is to achieve decoding thoughts and the inner voice and even dreams, a three-system function is mandatory. I argued that humans already have a two-function system where they have everything as double. The brain and nervous system we know and an identical but hidden secret internal system of which the inner voice is the clue we know. Thirdly, we must have an artificial one, a digital one that we can learn from, manipulate through electromagnetic nerve tampering and stimulation to be able to understand without doubt what people think at any given point and time.

If anyone is serious about robotics, I propose they use my invention which is the only way possible. All three systems in robots all digital as in artificial intelligence must work together as one see Fig 1 below.

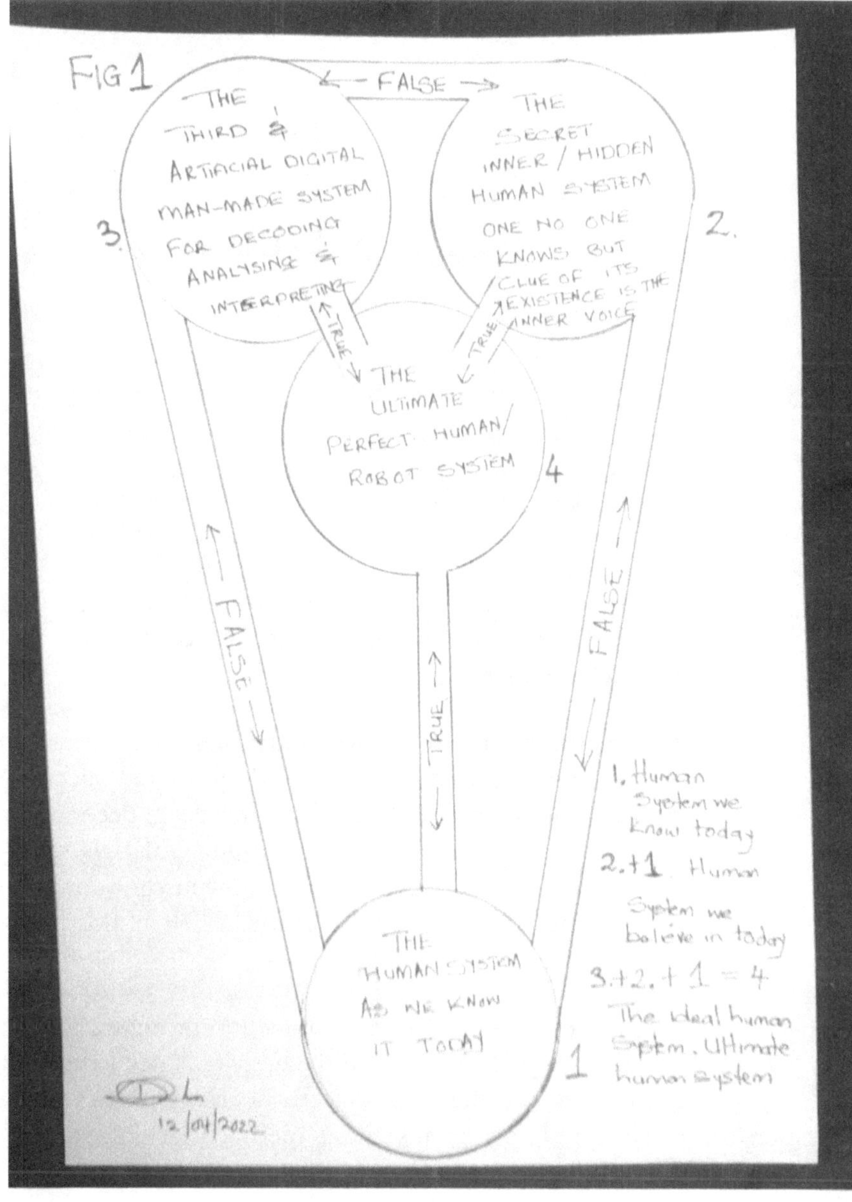
FIG 1
THE THIRD & ARTIFICIAL DIGITAL MAN-MADE SYSTEM FOR DECODING ANALYSING & INTERPRETING
3.
FALSE
THE SECRET INNER / HIDDEN HUMAN SYSTEM ONE NO ONE KNOWS BUT CLUE OF ITS EXISTENCE IS THE INNER VOICE
2.
TRUE
TRUE
THE ULTIMATE PERFECT HUMAN / ROBOT SYSTEM
4
FALSE
FALSE
TRUE
THE HUMAN SYSTEM AS WE KNOW IT TODAY
1
1. Human System we know today
2.+1. Human System we believe in today
3.+2.+1 = 4
The Ideal human System. Ultimate human system
12/04/2022

CHAPTER THREE

Debunking the so-called obstacles in decoding thoughts.

Difficulties in decoding thoughts.

The complexity of the brain is a hindrance to decoding thoughts.

The brain is so complex and connected and with billion neurons all linked together that it would be difficult to decode all these thoughts with modern techniques, etc.

All flawed current methods look at where the brain activity is occurring instead **of what neurons are firing**. I doubt a few electrodes or sensors on top of the brain would be able to make you decode thoughts etc. The functional magnetic resonance imaging FMRI is spatial and lacks the time part as in time-space. So on its own might not accurately identify the thoughts at the time in question. Then all this becomes a guess and eliminate-trouble shooting method.

The current methods look at areas of operation of neurons or activity within the brain. They identify where the activity is occurring and then try to map that area and the brain's electrical activity to decode what a person is thinking. That means these methods lacks the time-space requirement.

Current methods don't address the need to record both in space and time.

But do you know a brain is capable of thinking above six hundred thoughts per minute? We as humans think faster than we speak, which is around one hundred and fifty words per minute.

That means per minute that is in 60 seconds, a brain can think about 600 items; thoughts, images, memories, etc.

60 seconds is a long time and given the complexities of the brain, one can argue that it is difficult to know exactly what one is thinking unless a method is used that can measure in both space and time.

That alone renders all current methods obsolete or not fit for the task. All current methods fulfill one of the requirements, either fulfilling the space requirement as in the use of functional magnetic resonance imaging fMRI or the electroencephalography EEG that tries to measure the electric activity of the brain in terms of time.

A lack of a holistic approach to decoding thoughts.

Current methods don't link between the firing neurons, the space this occurs, the patterns produced and the intended actions or messages sent.

Misunderstanding of the structure and mechanism of the brain.

I argued in my first book; Thoughts To Word Or Audio, that the human body is so complex that we don't really know what it is made up of until now. The human body has two systems with one being a duplication of the main one, but one that works the opposite. You can say that the human system is a two-in-one thing. Yes, two mouths, two brains, two ears, two nervous systems, only that the other is a secret one that is internal to the body. In other words, it requires two people to communicate over the phone with each other, whereas a human system can do the same within itself. Once this is mastered, everything fits in place. The inner voice starts to make sense. This inner voice is the only clue to the fact that humans have double the systems with the inner one operating opposite. My arguments are that the human system is perfect. But all perfect systems according to Newton's Law, also have an equal but an opposing force. That means we have a mouth that speaks and a microphone inside that listens when we speak and sends messages in the opposite direction at the same time.

The mouth sends words outward (sound waves) to the recipient. A person we are talking to. Then another copy but as light waves is sent inward to the internal system.

Need for detailed studies, algorithms, and calibration in that people's neural connections differ greatly from a person to person.

Understanding human thinking is complex as more than 100 billion neurons are present and knowing which is responsible for what is a huge task.

Other things, like emotions and other experiences, can't be explained by simply looking at neurons.

But we have solutions to all this and my invention is the answer.

CHAPTER FOUR

Solving the difficulties of decoding thoughts.

1. Solution to complexities of the brain.

Decoding the neurons and mapping all these areas of the brain parts responsible for them, what they do and where they trigger spikes, and the kind of message they send if studied can overcome this difficulty. We now have faster and superior computers and technology that can easily map all these and categorize all the neurons.

Resolving the complexities of the human system.

I explained in the first book that my invention will work to resolve this issue. The needle diode Fig 1 in the first book page 43 must be used to relay the message sent by the brain and or nervous system and amplify these and then pass this message to the rotary propeller that uses electromagnetic waves to receive the message and then forward this message to an external translator or decoder.

First and foremost, I explained in detail in the first book the need for a classification system that will enable one to identify, encode, decode and be able to tell exactly what neurons are firing. I understand the nervous system when sending messages sends these as electrical waves that make click sounds that are specific to the message sent. Research has shown that these are specific for the message sent and or specific for identified aspects.

Meaning each sound can be linked to a specific aspect.

First therefore assuming time is spent collecting all these sounds together with other information like the host, the sender, the requester of messages, the responder of the messages, the type of the click sounds, the nodes and ports they pass through, and other aspects that can help to decode can all be collected over time.

Once that is done, then some kind of classification is needed to detect and differentiate the click sounds and these must be classified and linked to the alphabetical order from A to Z. Meaning each letter must be linked to a certain click sound.

The purpose of the electrode needle is a miniature representation of the spinal cord with sensors that correspond to nerves that exit or enter the spinal cord in the human body.

I explained in the first book the need to mark these areas and give them an identity that takes into consideration the area of the body responsible for that function, the possible requester of the message, the responder to that message, the likely path the message could travel, the likely encoding hash, the likely decoding hash, etc. The areas of the brain can be marked by numbers from 1 to 16 or more, depending on their functions.

The rotary propeller with magnetic properties to use electromagnetic waves acts as the receiver of the detected sound clicks from the needle electrode. The rotary propeller, as I said in the first book; should have a recording rotary disc that is first used to record the messages sent from the needle diode mainly through radio wave frequency identification (contactless). I mentioned in the first book that the means of communication between the electrode needle and the rotary propeller could be through wireless communication means with transmitters, etc. fitted on both.

The rotary discs record the noises sent as electricity.

The neurons when they send a message are converted at the synapses and this process, if measured, produces an electrical sound click that can be recorded. That is the sounds of neurons firing. The classification of these sounds and linked to the alphabetical order can be used as part of the holistic approach to decoding thoughts.

But care must be taken because it is not this simple in real life but practice and collection of information over time can help to decode the thoughts.

I think the reason why the human system is believed to have so many neurons' billions of them, is that information at first is in two ways. The forward message and the inward message. Meaning one is sent to the intended part of the body and a reverse one sent back inward or to the motor sensors to prepare the body for the intended next move.

Each message has a requestor and a responder rather than just having a sender.

To send the message, the body breaks down the messages into unique packets and assigns some form of identifying classification and sequencing of that message. Then some coding of that message for easy transfer and routing.

I believe that the message is split into smaller sound clicks that are sent over the network routes via certain ports of the central nervous system. But they are sent to specific areas of the nervous system where they are grouped according to type and compiled together.

Picture a chef assembling so many items from different sources but not making the dish himself but sending all these to another chef. First sending, everything as good as ready, meaning chopped onions separated into small amounts and sent via different channels depending on the time of cooking the other chef must add these. Not necessarily as the type like all chopped onions sent via the same route, etc. Here the onions can be referenced whether part of the frontend, the backend, their host, method of transport, the port they will pass, the encoding hash, or the decoding hash.

All items are referenced in line with the port they will pass and the specific port responsible for assembling these. The ports receive only the messages intended for that port and when received the message is assembled into batches from each port to the other as it is built until near the final destination where they are reassembled using the body's serial codes to make this message meaningful. The purpose of the rotary propeller recording disc is to record this message and assemble it to identify which neurons have fired the message, which areas of the body or brain are the intended receiver, the type of the message, etc. to decode the thoughts.

CHAPTER FIVE

A shift from emphasizing the inserting of sensors in the brain to aiming to get even more information from the nerves themselves to identify which neurons are firing.

A holistic approach will use the information above and automatically change the way neuroscientists think about this. Instead of looking at where the activity is happening, a case that requires some opening of the brain etc. which is a risk process. The very reason why people are skeptical about this as it involves some risks..

But a shift in thinking altogether about all this from looking at the place of activity to identifying what neurons are firing will reveal an even safer method that does not necessarily occur in the brain. You can attach a needle to the network of nerves in the body and be able to detect the kind of electric signals sent, where they originated from, and where they are being sent. Read the first book, Thoughts To Word Or Audio. The needle will represent the human system, making three systems part of the human body, as I argued in the first book, Fig 1. Now the body has three systems. The original system which we all know, its hidden internal system which the inner voice is part of, and our third artificial-digital one. One that is synchronized and matched to the body's hidden inner system to understand the body.

3. Delayed Time-Space Continuum Mechanism as a solution to the need to record both in space and time

The best method is one that records both in space and time to be able to pinpoint exactly what a person is thinking given that a brain is capable of thinking six hundred thoughts a minute or more.

I proposed in my book that the best accurate method is one that looks at the whole human system at a given point in time. The only way to do that is to create a third system and introduce this in the body to imitate the internal body's system, one inside; the hidden system. That means recreating everything a human body has.

A digital microphone or chip fitted to the magnetic rotary propeller as in my first book.

A digital speaker or chip that can be linked to a speaker.

A GPS tracker to pinpoint exactly the place and location and place the person in terms of space with coordinates and linked to the satellite system.

A recording magnetic tape or disc that will record and be accessed for playback issues.

A playback feature.

An antenna that will enable reception of signals and transmitting these.

A chip that can link to a computer

An infrared chip that can send or receive signals

An internal chip.

All this will enable the use of a scientific and physics principle in relation to Albert Einstein's theory of relativity referred to as the delayed time-space continuum mechanism where it is possible to revisit a place in time and know what happened then through the manipulating of the delay it takes for messages to be beamed down back from the satellites as the earth defects the path of satellites as they rotate around the end and the time it takes to beam the coordinates back the position of a place at a given time.

It is believed that there is a delay in relaying the message between occurrence and the time the satellites beam back this information to earth.

Manipulating this will enable the revisiting of a point in time and knowing exactly what happened at that time. Even makes it possible to recreate and combine or synchronize what happened to the current situation, which will enable us to make it look like the event is occurring at that very moment.

Why I'm skeptical about current methods is that they put sensors on top of the head and then claim to have recorded thoughts of a person when the area they have put sensors in is just a part of the brain in most cases not even involved in making that thought. FMRI does not point to brain activity at the very moment in time.

It is like putting sensors in the person's brain area responsible for hearing and then claiming to decode the vision of that person. I think it's a third type error. The methodology and aims are correct but it is like finding a solution but to the wrong problem.

Another issue is the misconception that you must place sensors in the brain to decode the brain. Isn't it wise to go to the nerves themselves and ask who the hell of the neurons, fired the neurons? I explained somewhere the need for recording both in terms of time and space.

My invention in the first book is the only one so far that records at the same time and space and where you can even manipulate the delayed time-space continuum mechanism to travel back in time and replay what was recorded at a given point that a person can hear what occurred at that point as if it was happening. This enables superimposing of events that occurred at a given point and time. Events that can be replayed as if happening now, then record everything to make it look like that person was at the first scene. This trick will enable several tests to be carried out with the same conditions repeated in near perfect situations so that the results are spot on. Imagine ten people doing exactly the same thing and checking all their brain activity at that point in time. You can confidently say that the results will be a true representation of what happened there. The only best solution to all decoding of thoughts methods.

This delayed time-space continuum mechanism makes it possible to record events at a point in time that can then be replayed back inside the person's ears so that it imitates the inner small voice.

This delayed time-space continuum mechanism makes it possible to record the inner voice and or imitate the inner voice where the four-dimensional points and the theory of relativity by Albert Einstein make it possible to record at different points and then use different frequencies to replay the recording so that a person can hear 'the inner voice'. A technique that can be used to insert the small voice deep into the ear tunnel of a person when sleeping and give instructions in that if it is in that person's voice the brain can convert this replay into the dreams of that person. When he wakes up he will think that he was dreaming all that.

This technique enables one to manipulate frequencies of different variations to recreate the inner voice that can then be converted into dreams with the person asked about the dreams when he wakes up. Then the brain activity patterns recorded by the optical inbuilt functional magnetic resonance imaging FMRI before all this being decoded to match the inputted inner voice turned dreams, what the person says and the decoding results from the simulation and algorithms. Making this a holistic approach.

This enables the recreation of events in four places at the same time. This will come in handy, as I explained in the first book. Where a third person is needed to be synchronized to the subject in such a way that whatever the subject does, the third person will do the same but as delayed in time-space in seconds or minutes but at a different but synchronized location. The person when linked to the subject but at a different location can have an inner voice (speaker) inserted into his ears tunnel that only he hears the voice or events of what is happening at the subject's location. This can enable two people if voices are matched between them. To have the inner voice played to all respectively. To make the message which is turned into dreams by the person's system. The purpose of the inner voice is to give the same instructions to both as they sleep. Later then test them in the morning after recording and decoding their brain activity. Then ask them what they have dreamt of. Then match this to what they have said; the inputted inner voice, and the decoded recorded brain activity. All this makes it easy to analyze everything using all this information and recreating standards and creating classifications e.g. identification system and stencils of alphabetical orders that can be used as references. Sound wave clicks etc that can be used to identify certain brain activity sounds etc. All this to be able to identify which neurons are firing.

Now we can do the reverse. We can now record the inner voice by inserting the place of the microphone inside the brain to record the inner voice. Not literally, but using the delayed time mechanism to move a point, to a point inside the brain where the voice can be replayed so that the person hears the small voice as if it was inside his head.

Brain activity is recorded at the same time, and the decoding methods are used to act as a second opinion. This is the only invention that makes it possible to have a second opinion, a third and as many as a thousand with a perfectly controlled environment in that the person can hear as an inner voice the subjects thoughts etc to replay this.

The amplifier comes in handy here, where the amplifier is used to record the inner voice and amplify this.

Another interesting thing you can do with a person is to use voice picking or recording software (software they use for order picking etc). The reason being that this software is person-specific in that it only works with your voice and no one else's.

The first step is to create a voice template for the subject. Make the subject speak in the microphone, words and numbers to create a voice template. The computer records this and stores this. Now you need an amplifier or a volume or frequency reducer that will lower the recorded voice to the levels of the inner voice. Where, like I said in the first book using the relativity theory, a point inside the ear tunnel is chosen and inserted inside so that the small voice played back there will be heard by the person as an artificial inner voice. This is possible, trust me.

At the same time, the brain activity is then recorded and mapped using all known decoding methods. All current methods can be used as second opinions and for comparisons. Other methods are used as well, as the shapes of the voice box and all the speaking systems, including the tongue's shape, etc.

The light waves produced as the person hears the artificial inner voice are recorded as well as the shape of the speaking system and the tongue etc, as in above.

(Note here that this invention is the only method that gives you the opportunity to recreate the inner voice which you know and play this and record brain activity associated with this then create stencils to use. A definite method. The only way to decode thoughts, inner voices and even dreams.)

Now ask the subject if he heard anything and what he heard. Now match everything; your inner voice stencil pattern, his brain activity, the neurons that fired etc to analyze, compare and know for sure what is what because you have control of everything. Trust me, never underestimate the power of this invention. One to change the world forever. If unsure, reach me welcome@gtps.finance.

The recorded and played back artificial inner voice.

The response from the subject to make sure the person heard the same thing as well as was played back.

Study the shape and pattern of the light wave shape recorded using functional magnetic resonance imaging. Use all methods and algorithms to decode this.

Another method can be used here using the needle electrode and the rotary propeller to measure the received electromagnetic waves and the vibrations they make at impact with body cells or nerves, etc. The vibrations can be measured and decoded as well, noting the sender and the requester, the frequency, etc. Note that frequency and energy are not lost in electromagnetic waves as it is absorbed and recreated before being sent to the next point.

All this with all other methods like the recording of memories, the training where the subject is trained through rigorous methods that use electromagnetic nerve wave tampering. See electromagnetic nerve tampering and stimulation. Where some needs and wants are limited so that the nerves fire constantly to be able to decode what nerves are firing, their position and the areas they send the messages to, etc.

All this is part of the holistic approach. I argued that to know exactly in the future what a person is thinking, you need to recreate and do some reverse engineering where you have control of the parameters, etc. Where you know for sure the initial inputs and the outputs are with a guiding reference to make sure that the system is perfect and output accurate.

The use of this delayed time-space continuum mechanism enables one to control the inputted variables and to know the outcomes. An artificial inner voice is created using the person's voice so that the brain won't reject the voice and frighten or wake up the subject. If a voice is the subject's own the brain is deceived to think it is him communicating with it that it can simply turn the dreams or the heard voice into part of the dreams so that the subject won't wake up but continue to dream about the replayed message.

All this practiced and repeated in different controlled environments will enable a sure way to predict and tell what a person is thinking and help decode the inner voice.

CHAPTER SIX

Rounding up the major points.

A holistic approach will enable the use of different methods to pinpoint exactly what a person is thinking.

The need to look at this Delayed Time-Space Continuum mechanism. We can use functional magnetic resonance imaging to record the space function that is required and combine this at the same time with the electromagnetic nerve interpretation, need to use the electroencephalography EEG and other mapping and algorithms and other lesion studies, etc.

A three-system approach must be adhered to understanding and decode thought. The human system must be viewed as having three systems, all in one. The human body includes the nervous system, the brain, nerves, neurons, etc. Another hidden system of the body is an equal and opposing force that acts in a reverse method with converted wave types. This means knowledge of all different waveforms is required. Waves here as well indeed act in twos, with one as an equal but opposing force, but one that acts in reverse. Meaning that if the sound wave is produced as speech, there must be another waveform produced at the same time, but in the opposite direction as light waves. Meaning instead of just an outward force, there is an inward force that is sent to the internal system as light waves. Or to motor sensors to prepare the body to move etc

That also means since we don't understand the inner hidden system of the body, a third digital system must be used as well to make us understand what goes inside the system. Making us be able to identify what exactly neurons are firing and the message sent, where it is happening and what the message is. This also enables us to measure or convert to electromagnetic waves the light waves in the body. The properties of the electromagnetic waves that are the opposite force as light waves will enable us to manipulate that to understand the neurons and their message. In that, the electromagnetic waves cannot be lost but will be absorbed by a body or object, etc., causing vibrations that can be measured or detected every time they hit the cells. The vibrations can be amplified to be detected and converted to interpret the waves and messages.

6. Here, current methods of brain mapping, computations, mathematical algorithms, and other computer simulations and algorithms are used to locate the areas of the brain where brain activity occurs. Detailed studies on the subject are to be carried out to know more about the subject. Read more in the first book, Thoughts to Word Or Audio.

Shapes and patterns of the voice box, the mouth, the tongue, jaws, etc. are measured and used to predict what a person is about to say. Language construction patterns and rules are used to identify what a person is thinking about. Brain imaging fMRI together with electromagnetic nerve stimulation and tampering, etc. are used to decode a person's thoughts.

A lot of algorithms and studies can be carried out with everything classified with the constructions of algorithms that interpret thoughts.

7. Advances in technology enable us to be able to create electric diodes that represent the body's spinal cord with sensory nerves and sensors representing the point of entry or exist of different nerves of the body in correspondence to different parts of the spinal cord and the part of the brain responsible for that.

8. Other experiences and emotions can be identified and observed through the use of electromagnetic nerve tampering and stimulation. Where the subject is subjected to experiments whereby starving is used to pinpoint areas of the brain responsible for that. As the need is not satisfied, the brain will cause spiking of neurons to send messages to the brain or body, for example, that the person must eat etc. if the

stomach is empty. The electromagnetic waves converted from light if intercepted and can be used to cause amplified vibrations to make parts of the body to be felt and or measured as vibrations.

CHAPTER SEVEN

Food for Thoughts.

I must say, writing these two books on decoding thoughts made me realize that all technological advancements and achievements since the beginning of time are just reverse engineering of the human system. Isn't that shocking, especially considering that up to now no one apart from me had come up with a convincing way of decoding thoughts when all technological advances after thorough research seem to have been derived from the human system?

Could we look at similar examples in the modern technological world and do reverse engineering and come up with even better methods that can help us decode not just thoughts and inner voices but also dreams, etc one day?

Donate if you can all our materials are free for use but if this works for you, you will be obliged to contribute back as well.

If you find this information useful donate generously PayPal davidgomadza@hotmail.com or digital currency to 0x50Deb1Aa94034f4f696Ac11e37d881d4F2B9a10f

Signed

David Gomadza

12/04/2022

Decoding Thoughts and Inner Voice
Explanations and Debunking the Misconceptions

ABOUT DAVID GOMADZA

David Gomadza is the President and Founder of Tomorrow's World Order. Founder of Gtps.Finance and the CEO. He is the author of several books namely;

<u>Thoughts To Word or Audio.: How To Know Exactly What Someone Is Thinking.</u>

<u>Tomorrow's World Order</u>

<u>Tomorrow's World Order: A New Law & Order. Dealing with Threats of Invasions, Wars and War Crimes</u>

<u>THE CONSTITUTION: [Official Edition] Tomorrow's World Order</u>

<u>Antitrust Laws The Case of Facebook v FTC TOMORROW'S WORLD ORDER'S PERSPECTIVE</u>

<u>Tomorrow's World Order Your Future Your Say: Executive Summary Edition</u>

<u>The New Laws</u>

<u>Tomorrow's World Order The Constitution : & Our Important Principles</u>

<u>Irredeemable Annuities: The Slavery Abolishing Act Of 1833: Forget what you heard! Let the truth be told.</u>

<u>The New Single Reserve Global Currency: FutureGoldCoin</u>

<u>Evelina The Alpha</u>

<u>Fortified: Defensive Training: Training To Build Massive Walls Around Vital Organs.</u>

<u>Evelina New World Order</u>

<u>Evelina The Omega</u>

<u>Evelina God's Dilemma Solved</u>

Decoding Thoughts and Inner Voice Debunking the Misconceptions

Leading all humanity to the next stage of development. A stage so advanced that we only need to look at a car for the car to drive off. Only need to look at each other and actually talk.

Are you ready?

I am.

Tomorrow's World Order.

www.twocoming.com

www.gtps.finance

welcome@gtps.finance

Decoding Thoughts and Inner Voice
Explanations and Debunking the Misconceptions